Levels

Love

Pain

Purpose

Peace

Poems

By

Felicia Nicole

Printed in the United States of America

ISBN 978-0-578-34142-0

Cover design: Travelin' Light Publishing

Published By Travelin' Light Publishing

Travelinlight.mg@gmail.com

This Book is Dedicated to my children; Nyasia, Koreem and Destiny.

To whom I owe my life for making me the woman I am today. To whom God chose me to give life to. The three people on this earth who has brought me the most joy and love. I will forever be thankful. I love you all without limits and fearlessly with every fiber of my soul and beyond this world.

I pray you all know that loving fearlessly is a true superpower. It's a love which is the purest love that can be given unconditionally. A love without limits or fear which is how I love you all. Greatness awaits you.

Fab 4 For Life

Love always,

Mama

Table of Contents

Fearless Love

To give love freely and without limits

is a sign of loving fearlessly, purely &

unconditionally.

That is my superpower to give a love so true it radiates
from my soul and penetrates you.

Through hurt and through pain

I still love over and over and over again.

I love Fearlessly because I am love.

I love deeply because I am unafraid.

A Piece of Me

Loving you required a piece of me.
A special piece of me. A piece that only you could feel, please
or see. A piece that was put deep inside of me for you to find
and give light to in my quiet, hurt and lonely times.

A piece that went dim in our times of strife, a piece that
shined brightly in our good times, like the day I became your
wife. The piece of me that went with you when we were no
longer one. I looked for that piece as it was essential to me
being me.

I searched high and low. I searched the stars at night, the
moon and the sun, until one night the piece came to me in
my dreams to let me know it was needed with you. Because
that piece of me made you a better you.

Rainbow

My love is like the colors of the rainbow.

The passion of red. Full of life and robust.

Sweet like the orange fruit picked fresh from a tree.

Soothing like yellow hue. It's calming like the sun setting on the ocean. Now that's a beautiful view.

Or it could be compared to the green hills that takes you away as far as the eyes can see, and your heart can go.

Can you see how my love is like the colors in the rainbow.

Do you like how this rainbow of love makes you feel?

See the power of the rainbow, its sunshine after the storm, is almost surreal.

Some days my hue is blue. On those days I'm not at my best, but I bounce right back like the Queen I am with my indigo & violet love crest on my chest.

My love is like the colors in the rainbow, with more to offer than just a pot of fool's gold.

My love engulfs your heart and soothes your soul.

This is the power of my love rainbow.

Damn Rain

The rain that washed away my pain felt like love hitting my skin. It tasted like pleasure washing away my sins. This Damn rain was cleansing my heart of loss love and past shame. Uhm this damn rain.

This rain had mixed with my tears to wash me and remove fears. To restore my faith in lost time that I would never get back because it was no longer mine.

Can you hear it? Can you feel it? Can you taste it? Rain. This damn rain, tap tap tap tap sounds like a love song on the windowpane. A song I'll keep on repeat. This rain has restored me, has me standing tall and strong on my feet. The rain has made me new. I'm smiling, winning and loving again. It could do the same for you.

I told you that's the power of that Damn Rain.

The Apology

The apology went like this.

I'm sorry you made me cheat.

What the hell did you just say to me?

I stopped, stood still, and looked him in the face. This man must be from out of space.

Wait, hold up, pause, press play, repeat. There must be something I'm missing. Is this really an Apology!

This must be a new kind of apology. One with a twist or could it just be I'm confused.

No, with a gleam in his eyes he said to me, didn't I say sorry, damn I apologized.

With tears in my eyes, I could feel the heat rising from my feet.

I replied, no sir keep that lame apology. That shit couldn't be for me. Furthermore, it's not accepted. You think that's the apology I deserve for the way I was disrespected. Ha ha you're a joke, a fool, a clown a whole minstrel show.

Now move on from me with that bullshit apology. You're dismissed YOU CAN GO!

The Sex

The way you sex me is on my mind.

Your lips, your kiss, your hands as they move between my thighs puts a curve in my back every time. Damn thinking of the sex makes me hot & wet. I long for you all day anxiously awaiting what you'll do to me next. I can see each encounter like a movie in my mind. I hear all the things you make me say, yes daddy its yours all day every day.

I have been taken to heights that I've never been. Mesmerized by the measures you go to please me. Yes, even your flow gives me chills. Strong, slow, hard, fast whatever it takes to please me.

The sex has me hypnotized; hands tied behind my back you win. The look in your eyes before kissing my sweet spot, what you call your chocolate filled honey pot. I can still feel your tongue rolling as you're tasting me and your strong hands holding me close, face deep in. You're making sure you taste every drop. Loving with your tongue with razor sharp precision. Damn what ya'll know about "The Sex."

Self-Apology

The apology to me...

I apologize for letting you get hurt, for not letting you see what you needed to see, instead of looking through rose-colored glasses and getting slapped by reality.

I apologize for letting you sit at a table where bullshit lies, and secrets were only on the menu. No character, no substance, no love, no integrity, no character. No humanity.

I apologize for allowing you to believe part of you had to die for that man to be who he needed to be.

I apologize it took so long for you to understand and see that he wasn't for you

Mentally emotionally spiritually.

He wasn't on your team. He saw you as a threat, his competition, not his Queen.

I apologize that you didn't recognize he was a wolf in disguise, and you were too much for him. He'd rather pull you down than be a man and rise to meet you at your level of love and greatness.

Do you forgive me?

Apology accepted. I'm glowing, I'm winning, I'm loving, I'm free.

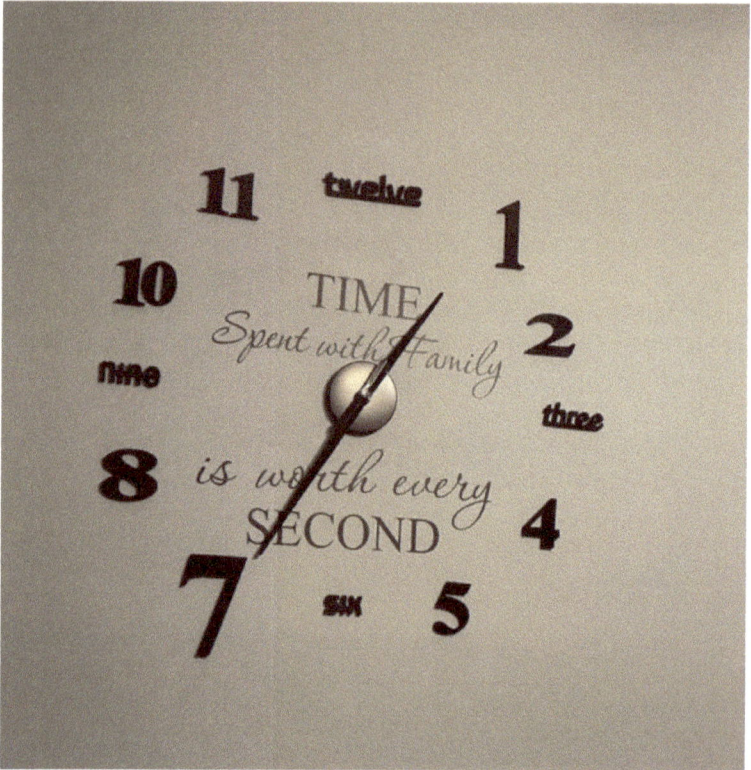

The Hands of Time

Looking back @ the hands of time

My life's eye. The essence of what was, and what will be.

How once it's gone it never comes back to me.

How important is my time?

Too precious to waste, so easy to lose and too valuable to give away.

I'm mindful and cautious with time not to play.

Not to waste it, not to squander it. I'm thankful for each minute, each second of the day.

The hands of time waits for no one. Blink and time lost with the rising of the sun. A new day begun. More time.

Hold on to the hands of time. Enjoy what time you're given, never take time for granted. You'll look up one day & the hands would have stopped and there's no more time to be given, wasted or taken for granted. It's what most regret.

You look up, and your time has come to an end.

Sister, Sister

Sister, sister they are the links in my chain.

Its only right you know them by name.

The women that know me best. My gang, gang, gang.

The ones who I share all my secrets. They know what makes me laugh, what makes me cry, what brings me to tears and my darkest fears. I can go to them when I have something on my chest, when I'm being a bit extra, they know me well enough to say, it could be you sis now take a deep breath.

I lost one of my sisters & I lost a piece of me that day. Lisa is her name. I speak of her in the present tense for me in my heart she remains.

I'm still grieving her passing, a part of me is missing.

I love you sister sister

My other ladies, my sisters my gang gang gang.

There is Sonia Atiyah, Kenya, Ladeanna, Monica, Tammy, Lenora, Polly and Monique. Wendy and Juanita, Camille, Rasheeda ET, and Christine. I trust them with my life no if ands or buts. I've never questioned if they got me their loyalty is absolute.

I gave them my heart. Trust they are my riders, my sisters my friends from dawn to dusk. We've laughed, cried, loved together and even mourned. We're in this till the end.

Sister, sister my love for you is so true it scares me at times to think of losing another one of you. I could go on but it's not necessary. Just know I'd go through the fire with you and for you. I'd kick in any door, yes sis you know me waving the 44

Put this on everything don't let the necessary occur!

Sister, sister.

No Shame

There's no shame in pain.

It's something we all go through.

It's what makes me, me and what makes you, you.

We are made and forged from pain.

When two become one in a passion filled night of love making from dusk to dawn.

The pain from passion bonds us forever more.

There's no shame in pain, from the pain we grow.

It's the foundation of who we become.

We can run from the pain or to it.

If we run, we'll never learn to get through it.

No shame in pain.

Healed.

You'll Love Again

You'll love again…

I know through the tears, the hurt and pain you don't believe it's possible to love again. You doubt there's true love in the world. Let me tell you that's just the pain talking.

Trust me sister you will survive this just like me.

 I lost a love, but I found it again. But it wasn't in a man. The love I found was the love of self from deep within.

Loving you must come first. So, forgive yourself then pamper yourself. Look at her in the mirror. Wow she's beautiful and loving her won't hurt. You'll love again after you love you first.

That love will make you stronger. Loving you will attract the right kind of man who will love you, respect you, and support you through whatever.

You'll love again. Your season is coming, life gets better.

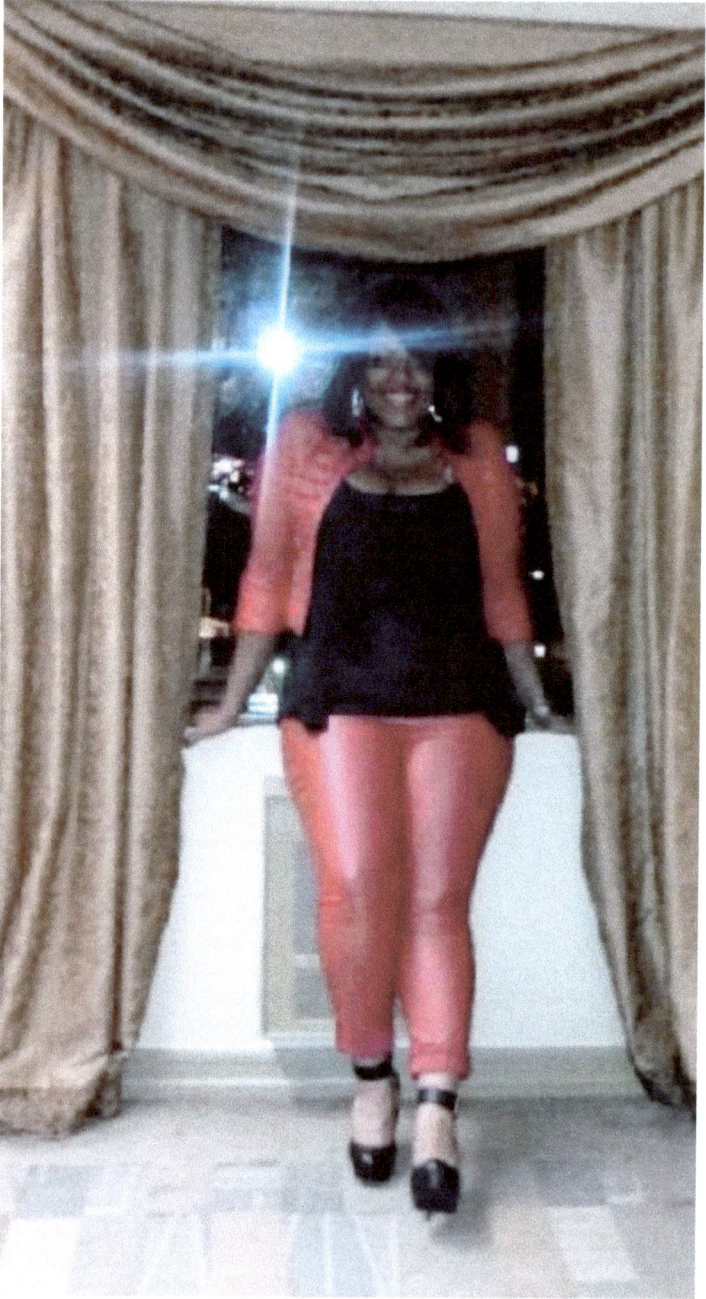

I Love My Damn Self

I love my damn self

I'll treat my damn self

I'll encourage my damn self

I'm so beautiful

I'm capable

I'm enough

I'm strong

I'm ready

to love my damn self.

I Was Ready

I was ready for a family; I was ready to be a wife.

While you were seeking attention from the community. Coming home causing pain, misery, discord and strife with all your lies.

I was ready to do whatever for our forever.

But your cheating ways pushed me away. I almost fell victim to an imaginary life with you, living in purgatory if you had your way.

 I woke up just in time with no regret because I was ready.

This I know to be true; I was ready and gave my best to you.

When the right one comes along I'll be more than ready, and that kind of love is long overdue.

I am ready to do what I must do.

Are you

A Price to Pay

My belief in you almost cost me, ME.

That was a price too high to pay.

There's no dollar value or price high enough to pay for losing me.

My belief in you almost cost me, ME.

I was busy building, believing, and supporting you while you were busy plotting to tear me down. You wanted to destroy me.

I was stronger than you expected.

Now I'm gone, disconnected.

A price too high to pay.

I gave love a home, a place you were protected

that you threw away, neglected.

Can you handle the price you paid now that you've lost me?

Was it all worth it? The life I offered was priceless.

You chose to play now you pay.

The price.

What Makes Me, Me?

What makes me, ME?

My eyes, my lips, my smile.

My hips, my thighs, my soul and this heart of mine.

The intricacy of my mind's eye.

And how all the parts work harmoniously together to form a symphonic melody of me.

A melody, a sweet rhythm only a pure heart can see what makes me, ME.

My laugh, this round ass and plump breast.

This smart mouth and brilliant mind.

Is it how I cross my T's or how I dot my I's?

Could it be all these things combined?

I think it's how I give love without fear or condition that sets me apart.

 Yup it's this heart that makes me, Me.

Close your eyes; pump, pump listen to this love flow and move through this chest.

Yup that's what make me, Me.

I'm forever harmonious.

She Changed Me

She changed me…

No, she saved me at 16.

God knew I needed her, so he chose me.

He sent Nyasia Monique to be my first baby

She was for me. Sent by God Herself

So beautiful, my sweet baby girl, like a doll off a shelf.

She came and calmed my angry, broken heart.

I knew it was eternal love from the start.

I knew the day our hearts connected they would never part.

She changed me and saved me.

I was walking around in pieces, a mess.

Then 10-7-1989, my life was forever blessed.

With an angel in my arms that would change my world.

She changed me. She saved me.

My Nyasia, The Queen Bee, My sweet baby girl, My lifeline, My reflection, My legacy.

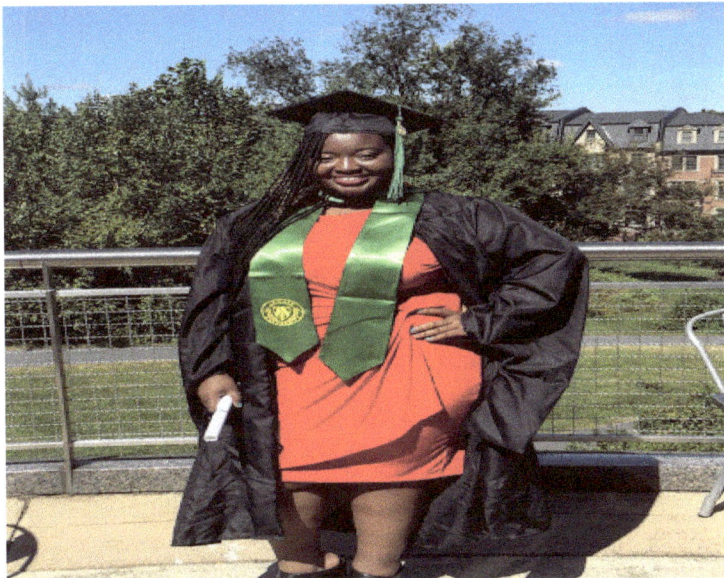

The Man God Sent to Me

The man God sent to me passed through me to shine love from my soul for eternity.

My King, My Sonshine, My Baby, The Gift. I call him many names.

Only God knew I would birth a young King. Koreem, AKA Poppy.

He is Lion "born to" protect, never to neglect the lioness in his life. He's a great man filled with love, honor and integrity.

Yes, he'll forever be my baby.

A man of his word, of faith and great morals and character.

He's the one man who always has my back.

My eyes and heart fill with love and pride awaiting the day he's a father and… with his own family to guide

The man God sent me, that came through me. I call him my one and only son.

He added another level to me the day he was born.

He took the lessons of one life and multiplied; this young King is the leader of our tribe.

The man God sent me came through me, My one and only son

A love for eternity.

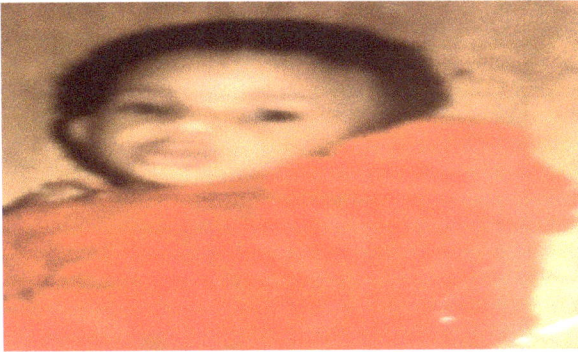

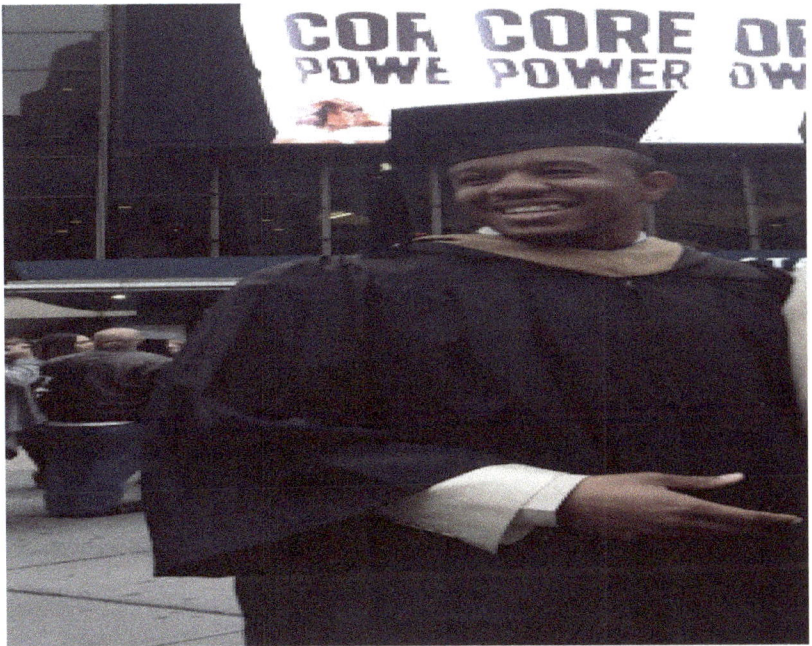

My Destiny

She's my Destiny

The one who brought a new meaning of life to me

She came at a time of life's new beginnings.

God knew she was what I needed to get back in it (Life, land of the living).

Having her saved me. She gave me a purpose, my fighting spirit.

A new drive

More strength

A new power from within. My Destiny.

My love, my rainbow baby came to restore and rebuild me. Restore, replenish

My Destiny

So sweet, a kind heart, pure sprit, genuine love yes that's it.

I see the best part of me when I look at you.

My Destiny

My cookie dough, My Tootie, My Pooh.

You're one of God's angels on Earth who he created just for me.

My sweet girl, My light, My heart, My world,

My Destiny.

Pissed

I have a right to be angry

I have a right to be pissed

Trying to lift you up and hold you down

Be your ride or die, your down ass chick

Left me with opportunities missed.

I have a right to be angry

I have a right to be pissed

You were out here serving the community like you're a got-damn politician with your penis.

Out there lying, cheating all kinds of shit.

I have a right be angry

I have a right to be pissed

But I'm good now, best of luck to you.

Peace and blessings to you and yours, new bitches, old enemies, and your side chick.

When the Mask Fell Off

When the mask fell off, your betrayal cut deep.

You were like Brutus to my Caesar, my enemy.

I let my guard down to let you in, then your mask fell off.

My eyes wide open trader, my homie lover friend.

Unbeknownst to me I had been sleeping with the enemy.

The charade was up, you could no longer pretend to be the man you portrayed yourself to be.

When the mask fell off it broke my heart.

I was mad at myself

I should have seen through your act from the start.

Phantom of the opera that's who you are.

It was destined for your mask to come off because we had to end. I'm out here winning; you're out here faking your life.

It's make-believe, you like to pretend.

The blessing was the day your mask fell off.

Beat

I'm in pain some days from the top of my head to the soles of my feet.

Feeling like, on those days this life shit got me beat.

I fall, I rise

I fall, I rise

Grey to blue skies hurting with tears in my eyes.

I tell myself on those days a little mantra I like to repeat

Get your ass up

Stand on your feet.

Do you know who you are? You're not beat.

You a got-damn Queen? This is your life not a movie.

No more feelings of shame, no more feelings of guilt

You're a rare breed

For this life shit, yes sis you were built.

Good or bad, stand tall

One day at a time

You don't have to fix it all

Move slow to the beat of your own drum.

Beat

The Request

"Never give up on me"

Was that a joke or a request?

From where I'm standing, you gave up on your damn self then tried to place that responsibility on My chest.

Never give up on you, Lord knows I tried my best.

You were Pandora's box to me.

I had to suffer like Epimetheus because of Prometheus fucking with Zeus and his vengeance.

But like Pandora's box, there's no hope for us.

So, take your request Shove it down your throat.

Then Kiss my ass make that request your last.

Elusive Love

Sometimes the elusiveness of love is painful when you're searching in a sea where there's no loyalty.

The delusion of the illusion of an all-inclusive type of love is just a fantasy.

We search the depths of our souls and hope that this can't be.

There must be more out there in the sea.

Love elusive this can't be.

The world we live in, the normalcy of infidelity, the acceptance of being a proud side piece.

Elusive love where are you? So many lost spinning in the wind.

Love out here what's real or what's pretend

Love lost, love hope, love fake, love new

Elusive love where are you?

Aiding and Abetting

Look at you, look at you

Out here looking sick.

Things didn't turn out like you thought with them side chicks.

Instead of taking care of home and building a connection,
you looked in the mirror and didn't like your reflection.

You had these side chicks aiding and abetting.

Cosigning the falsehood of the man you pretended to be.

Silly fools helping you promote the fallacy of a family man, a
good husband and daddy.

Aiding and abetting was their crime not mine. I let that ass go
I had done my time.

Love Birds

I want a love like the Scarlet macaw or the bald eagle.

One that soars and lasts forever, two equals.

A love that speaks without words.

When he moves, she moves tranquil.

A love that's majestic, harmonious, transparent.

You know effortless, see through.

No lies no games just true love.

Love birds, lovers for life,

The beginning, the end, no sequel.

Links in My Chain

You are the links in my chain, the pieces linked together to form who I am

The links in my chain

Mommy, Daddy

Sister, Brother

Aunty, Uncle, Cousin

Best Friend

My family

The links in my chain

Tightly woven

If one breaks, we're strong the bond remains

The links in my chain

1989,1992, then 2008 a new link came

Nay, Pop Des you are the links in my chain

Piece by Piece

I want you to taste me and consume me, piece by piece.

Start from my toes, move to my ankle, then slowly move up my legs to my thighs.

Take your time, nice and slow for an orgasmic release. I shudder and close my eyes.

 I need you to know every inch, every part of me.

As you move up, I hold my breathe before you go inside me. With your finger first you tease me, and I beg you to stop

My back curved, just so you can hit my g-spot.

Make my legs quiver and my body shake

You move in with your tongue sucking me

Licking slow caressing my clit.

I'm about to erupt, orgasm reached, a tear roll from my eyes

You were getting to know me piece by piece.

You took your time to please me, to love me, to get to know me inch by inch, piece by piece.

Tonight, forever etched in my memory.

Fuck You

Fuck you

Fuck you yesterday

Fuck you today

Fuck you tomorrow

Fuck your hats

Fuck your job

Yes, fuck everything about you.

Fuck the way you walk

Fuck the way you breathe

Fuck the way you talk

Yes, I said what I said

Fuck you and that's from my heart

Fuck the way you chew

Fuck the way you live

Fuck everything about you

Just in case you don't understand, Fuck you.

Down Ass Chick

It don't make you a down ass chick if you're with a man for years that treats you like shit

That makes you his fool sis

A doormat

A got-damn puppet

It don't make you a down ass chick because he pays all your bills.

If that man left you today, what's your next move? Nothing, it's all downhill.

It don't make you a down ass chick cause he gave you a ring

That man still in those streets doing his thing.

Get yo ass up and open your eyes, a down ass chick? You're a damn dummy.

Don't you understand he aint down for you boo?

Being his ride or die, down ass chick was his plan and your demise.

Blade

The blade that's sharp on both sides

We're hurting each other without real reason

Why?

The blade is so sharp buried deep inside, egos so big no compromise.

We'll lose each other and a part of ourselves in the end

Look into my eyes, see the pain we've caused.

The blade is sharp on both sides.

Blade removed, it's all been lies, hurt and pain on both sides.

Damn too late we've committed relationship suicide.

The blade that's sharp on both sides.

Sunrises and Sunsets

Have you ever watched a sunrise or sunset through the eyes
of someone you love? Priceless

How about a moon lit night together? Perfect moment is a
vision of love.

Have you tasted the rain off the person-you-love's skin?

It intoxicates you like overproof gin.

Has just the thought of the person you love made you smile?

You love them so much it brings tears to your eyes.

You can smell them even when they're not there.
They've left they're love with you; it lingers in the air.

Sunrises and sunsets begin and end and look all the more
beautiful with you here.

Lie

You never had to lie to me

You never had to cheat

All you had to do was come talk to me like the man you were supposed to be.

Say you were unhappy; you didn't feel like our house was a home.

Instead, you chose to Lie

You took the coward way out

Moved your shit when I wasn't home.

Calling me at 6AM, "Good morning, baby," like it was a fucking joke.

Had me thinking, Is he on drugs? What the hell did he smoke?

Now you're back with more lies and pleas, how you want me back.

Here's the truth to match your lie you don't want me

I'm what you need

We should have never been

You were never my love you were just a fill in

That's the truth I have no room to lie goodbye.

A Lesson for My Son

When he was small, I had to teach him about being a man on my own.

I was his mom though, not sure of the outcome

But I told myself, "Do the best you can."

He got into trouble one day with a friend

On that day, the lesson of responsibility would begin.

I held him tight, looked in my baby boy's eyes and

said, "What did you do?!" as my hands met his thighs

He replied, "It wasn't me! It was my friend, Johnny!"

As hands met thighs a few more times and tears in both our eyes

I knew what I had to teach him

I said, "Little boy, repeat after me

I'm taking responsibility for what I do,

Not my friend,

Not my mom,

Not my sister."

Through tears, "If, I'm there while you do bad, I'm guilty too."

I had to teach him to be a leader

Not a follower

Not to be led astray.

If you're down to do a bad deed, there's a price to pay

Money won't save you when you've done wrong.

You must take responsibility like a man and accept the bad shit you've done.

 Correct it, then move on my son.

I can now say he is a great man.

Educated, responsible, hardworking, a leader.

The man of the family all because I told him take the responsibility.

A lesson to my son that day formed the man we both knew he could become.

Romeo

Social media Romeo

Social media pimp

Wish I could go back in time,

To the day you were in my DM's.

Had me laughing and smiling to all those lies you were telling.

Bullshit sweet words and half-truths, you missed your calling.

You're an actor, a clown a damn fool.

Damn social media Don Juan

I should have seen straight through you.

You're a social media Romeo & Social media pimp

It was easy, online, for you to pretend.

You couldn't keep up the fake charade you created

And it soon would have to come to an end.

Social media Romeo social media pimp

Grow the fuck up and stay out of chicks DM's.

He Showed me Love

He Showed me Love

He showed me what love was

Not that he told me everyday

It was the small things he did daily, very quietly and subtly, that showed me he loved me in a special way.

He showed me what love was by the way he looked at me and the way he touched my hair.

He'd kiss my forehead and my cheek, then he'd say, things like "Baby, did you eat?"

Don't worry I'm on my way.

"Pay attention to the little things," my granny would say. "It's how they show you they love you, never just what they say."

His love language spoke to my whole heart and captured my soul.

With him I finally knew love.

He showed me and told me what love was.

Levels

There are moves to be made when you want to get ahead.

Levels

Challenges will come to block your ascent.

Levels

Each new win will bring a new sin, a devil dressed like a friend.

That goes with leveling up.

Shit just keeps happening. Don't be wary and don't fret always remember its levels to this shit.

Levels

Don't lay down and never give up

Tomorrow's a new day to go at it again, keep moving level up.

Levels

Melanin

Was it this sweet brown skin that drew you in?

That's the power of Melanin.

To the way it tastes on your tongue that makes you want it even more.

Yes, that's the power of this sweet cocoa called Melanin

A blessing from the sun.

Not even the hands of time can disturb or define this Melanin.

Ageless

Not even a fine line can define or separate Melanin.

Priceless

How the sun dances off this magnificent skin, it's like gold Melanin.

Melanin has brought men to their knees.

Girl, do you know the power within is your melanin?

You're a brown skin Goddess that's who you are

Women pay for what you've been blessed with.

So, stand and be proud, spin around and love the skin you're in. Take a bow and let them bask in your glow.

Your Melanin.

Hot Chocolate

He called me his Hot Chocolate

Because of how I made him feel

Nice and warm on the inside, my sweetness going down his throat.

My Hot Chocolate was so good, once he got a taste that was all he wanted.

He was hooked on me, there was no cure or antidote.

All he thought about was his Hot Chocolate

That's what he called me his Hot Chocolate,

His baby, his lady.

Sweet Chocolate Latte

My Sweet Chocolate Latte was just what I needed

Strong, sweet, a protector, a grown ass man.

He said, "If you fall, I'll catch you." He believed in me.

He wasn't in these streets fucking with everybody. He called me his lady; said he'd never lie to me.

I'll never hurt you baby.

Skin so smooth and smile as bright as the sun.

Did I mention how he loved me down, stroked me with his tongue? At the end of the day, we knew it what it was.

He was mine and I was his, we didn't care what anyone had to say.

We gave zero fucks

My Sweet chocolate Latte gave me sweet love every day.

Not a tall Not a Grande

My Sweet chocolate Latte

He makes my heart skip a beat and my legs shake

For him I'd do anything.

He inspires me to push pass my fears, he nourishes me and enriches my mind.

I drink his knowledge. My Sweet chocolate Latte I am his and he is mine.

Quiet Storm

My Quiet Storm

A strong, quiet man that hardly spoke.

When he spoke, he spoke softly yet sternly.

His words never lost in translation, a Quiet Storm.

With kind eyes, A mild spirit, he was mine and I was his.

He didn't need to speak much, there was power in his touch.

How he moved, and all he did. He was a Quiet Storm our love short lived.

He was a superhero to me, he believed he was what Heaven could be.

He came into my life like a rainstorm on a summer day.

A smooth breeze, a light mist. A Quiet Storm, the kind you stand in and let the rain fall on you. You don't mind getting drenched.

My quiet storm, you are my regret.

The man I lost, the man I miss.

I Forgive You

I forgive you, but not for you

I forgive you for me and my peace,

Because I loved you and realized some of the blame rested on me

I'm not perfect, and neither are you

We out here hurting each other like we got beef and points to prove

I forgive you, now we can go on with our lives

Living and loving and building

Not as enemies just two people that had loved but ended up on different sides

I forgive you

Odds

What were the odds that I'd survive?

Not only did I survive, but I thrived

What was meant to break me made me see.

God placed me here to fulfill a great destiny

The prophecy of me was to live my mark on the world, a never-ending legacy

The statistics on my ability to survive were low

The odds against me were high

But I serve a merciful God that placed a higher calling on my life

My faith was so strong, I said, "What odds?"

What were the odds I'd survive? 0-10

The odds stacked against me were high

I'm surrounded by angels my elevation was the assignment

I saw no odds on what was meant for my life and all that God supplied

The odds were on my side.

Scared to Sleep

I was scared to sleep, the nightmares paralyzed me

Flashes of a faceless monster haunted my dreams

He made me touch him, then he'd touch me, this was a secret
I was supposed to keep.

I'd try to wake myself inside my mind was locked

I'd lay there and I'd pray, ask God to wake me up and to tell
him stop.

 I wanted to escape how could I get away

Sleeping with night lights to scare the monster away.

Have you ever been scared to sleep because you had a
Boogieman waiting for you in your dreams?

I prayed and asked God for one of us to die

He never answered, He gave no reply.

Why did he want me to suffer? I was scared to sleep so afraid
to close my eyes.

Then the boogieman died in real life, and I cried.

I would sleep for the first time in my life I thanked God and
that night I slept without the night light.

My prayers had been answered God had heard my cries.

No longer was I scared to sleep.

Child Molester

Child Molester, you are a killer of spirits

A thief of innocence, a predator

A child molester

You're a Boogieman that comes to steal what is pure

You're a cancer in society for you there's only one cure

DEATH

You're a child molester

I asked God to cleanse my heart of hate to help me find peace

Deliver me some justice, your suffering was what I prayed.

To know you suffered in the end pleases me. For you, just fate.

I often wondered since you knew my memory of you was well intact

Of all you did to me the heinous acts.

In your last days did you dream of me as you descend to Hell for all eternity,

Child molester

My Dreams at 16

I dreamed of better days

I'd just had a baby, I was now somebody's mommy.

She needed me to be the very best I could be,

To protect her and provide

This little angel was my legacy.

My dreams at 16 were to fulfill a prophecy that I'd be great,

To give my baby a fighting chance to make her mark on this world.

My dreams at 16 would come true

I look back and smile so thankful he kept his promise to never forsake me.

He carried me though to see my dreams from 16 become a reality.

I'm to Blame, It's My Fault

I'm to blame, it's my fault I forgave you

I put my trust in you, then you turned around and betrayed me like Bitch, I'm gonna do whatever the hell I want

 Now who the fuck are you? Gloves off.

I kept telling myself, yes, it's my fault, because I had the power to put the shit to a screeching halt, I didn't.

All the promises and sweet words were all just lies

It amazes me how calm you were while looking me right in my eyes.

No remorse, no regret

So self-assured in yourself and all your bullshit.

I'm to blame, it's my fault but this shit is over

Bye clown you're a fucking joke.

Mother, I Forgive You

Mother I forgive you,

Because I love you, I love you,

You're my mother, my earth

I believe you did your best with all the pressures you were under

You had to be a good daughter, be a good wife, be a good mother

There was nothing left for you to enjoy in life

You lost yourself in another

You tried your best to hide the pain, but you were smothered and it's no wonder you found an escape in drugs, a prison you were lost for years

Prayers to God that you'd recover

So much lost time, so much to say

But I forgive you, Mother

I love you and remember the good days, they outweigh all the bad. I remember all your sacrifices, your struggles, times when you were sad

You did a good job, Mommy Don't feel bad

Your babies made it, because the foundation was strong.

That foundation, you laid it I forgive you I love you,

Because you're my mother my earth.

Karma

Karma came to see me, and we had a conversation

We discussed all the bad I had done

I laughed and called Karma, Stacy

Karma replied this is no joke

Sis you about to catch all the smoke, it's your time to pay up

My debt was due Karma said, this will be swift and painful too

No one is exempt we all must pay the price in the end

Karma is efficient, methodical she ain't nobody's friend

You can't beg, borrow or plead when Karma comes for you her cuts are sharp and swift, we bleed

Karma won't kill you, you may wish for death

She opens your eyes; Karma comes to us all be patient but don't hold your breath

Karma

Second Time Around

Does he deserve a second chance?

A second chance to hurt me

A second chance to disappoint me

A second chance to show me he's a better man

He said he'll do all he can with his second chance

"I won't regret it, he said. I'll show you."

Second time around

I'll pass one time around was enough for me boo boo.

Other Woman

Phone rings, the other woman.

"Hello"

"Yes, hello if I may Id like to speak to you and please listen to all I have to say."

I hung up stunned and waited for my husband. Today was going to be a big day.

He walks in, I smile and say I spoke to your other woman today. My husband, "other woman?" "Yes, she surprised me with what she had to say."

Before you lie and deny

This other woman had text, pics, and receipts she didn't have time to waste or play.

She said you made her feel special, told her you loved her every day, and how you sent sweet texts like, "Good morning, beautiful. Did you eat and How was your day?"

The other woman said, I need you to know about me. I ask why

What he does with you is of no consequence to me

You chose your role as the other woman and that's what you'll remain to be.

A Fall from Grace

Sister, why is it that you're feeling less than you are

Is it because you're the one left with internal and emotional scars?

It hurts me to see this pain and loss on your face,

Believing that man leaving you was a fall from grace.

A fall from grace?

How could that be?

You are a remarkable, irreplaceable, and beautiful Queen

Look at you, you're a model brilliance you're a beast.

I shudder to even think you believe you've had a fall from Grace because of his mistake.

His loyalty was misplaced it is his loss he never deserved you in the first place. Truth be told, it's his

Fall from grace.

Free Love

Love is free

Free Love

I bet you didn't know that, as it seems like we pay a high price when we lose it or love too much. When you realize love is free, you are free to love genuinely unconditionally.

Free love

Love is free

Love Jones

Have you ever had a Love Jones?

A love that's embedded in your skin

A love you felt deep down into your bones

That's a Love Jones

It consumes you, becomes a part of your DNA

A love you never want to lose or be taken away

That Love Jones drives you insane

You can smell the one you're Jonesing for, even when their miles away

There's no distance far enough to break the love or bond

You can hear their laugh, see the gleam in their eyes

They're in your dreams, scenes of your love making sensuous and wild.

Love Jones is love that transcends time.

Words from a husband

Words from my husband

I don't need a mother, I need a wife

I had a mother that loved me like no other

She raised me to be a good man

I need you to understand I need a wife not a mother

That role was already taken

Your role is to Stand with me as we build

I'll provide and do all I can to lead our family

I need your belief in me with you I need solidarity

When things get rocky, I need you to hold tight not quit on me

Baby, I'm asking you to trust me and do your part, not as my mother but as my wife, the holder of my heart

I don't need a mother; I need a wife to love until death do us part

My misses, not my mother, but as my wife

I Believe We Can Make It

I know I fucked up, but I believe we can make it

Losing you is not an option that will be considered or taken.

You are my wife, My lover, My best friend

I stood before God, our family and friends.

I vowed only death could end this and that's what I meant

Yes, I know I fucked up, but we can make it.

I'm changing everyday into the man you deserve.

Whatever I need to do will be done for us to make it that's
my word.

I believe we can make it that's all I know.

I'm sorry I forgive you, but I'm gone my dear I know we
won't.

Get It

I get it

I sit back thinking and dreaming

I reflect over time and now, I finally get it

It took me a long time, and since I'm so smart, it's quite pathetic

You are a hater,

A scavenger,

A vulture,

And I was your prey

You preyed on my heart tried to pick me apart

I sit back and think, like damn now

I get it

Kiss

A morning kiss is like the sunshine that starts a new day

Morning kisses takes that pain from yesterday away.

Kiss me before you leave and when you come home each day.

Kissing is part of my love language I love your lips what more can I say.

I love to kiss your sweet Lips, your hard chest and your special spot the on the back of your neck. It's tender there, you always say stop baby don't start you know that's my spot.

Kiss, kiss, kiss, kiss, kiss

Good morning, good night kiss

Real Man

Have you ever been loved by a real man?

Loved so good it shakes you to your core, a love that overtakes you, envelopes you, wash over you, leaves you wanting more.

He does all he can for you and never shall his love fade

Never makes you wonder about his loyalty or where is heart belongs.

Real man, bills paid, keeps you laid right every night.

Have you ever been loved by a real man?

It's a love you grow old with together till a tender old age. He's there on every level, there when you turn a page.

The lovemaking hits just so right he takes his time makes sure you're pleased; he never rushes he's meticulous can go all night.

This man will be the love of your life.

It's the little things like washing your hair, protecting you every moment, you'll be happy enjoying life. The real man down on one knee asking you to become his wife.

The Vows

The vows I made and said to you were from my heart.

I vowed to love, honor, respect, until death do us part.

It seems like the vows were missing essential parts, like "I vow to help you, I vow to support you, I vow to uplift you, I vow to never forsake you or try to break you" yeah that part.

When we took those vows, standing before God, family, and friends, so happy not thinking how fragile they were.

The vows

They're more powerful than just the man or woman.

It wasn't until they were broken, their true meaning began to sink in and what that stood for or meant to me.

The lost of my friend. The vows were now our undoing.

Lost Mother

Lost Mother, lost but at what cost.

You see, Mother died she committed suicide.

She died not of the physical, but of the spiritual and mental Mother lost her mind and her pride.

Lost Mother, mother I knew was everything to me.

Brains, beauty, class, everything a mother was supposed to be.

Love, unconditionally.

The absolute epitome of what Wonder Woman was to me.

Lost Mother, lost to the streets. Its allure grabbed her, and she forgot about her babies. The streets and drug industry lied to her; she wasn't ready. It took her beyond the sky. Bye mother, lost mother died.

Lost Mother, lost when she chose drugs over her babies, the drugs were all that mattered to her daily. She chose drugs over if they had a place to sleep, food to eat or if we lived or died.

Lost Mother, lost to the world suicide.

Are You, My Father?

Are you my father or just the man that laid with my mother,
produced a child, then walked away?

You had time to play, but not time to stay,

Are you, my father?

Did you help with homework?

Take me to the park or help me when I was hurt?

Did you protect and provide, or wipe tears from my eyes?

Are you, my father?

The role model for the man that was to come after

My first tears, father

My first hurt, father

My first loss, father

The first man to let me down, father

Are you my father or the man that laid with my mother?

Made a child then walked away.

Seven

The significance of seven is not simply a number for me.

Its meaning of completeness and perfection… life to me not just the spiritual and physical but mentally.

I represent my seven as my day of birth

My DNA is … earth from my womb

The significance of seven is so strong, I manifested it

3 times 3x7=21, that's for me, both daughters, and my son.

My reality, my love you know who you are the God

The knowledge that manifested the completion of my heart.

Seven

You're My Hero

I was walking past a mirror the other day and there I saw her.

Hello beautiful long time no see I hadn't seen her in a while, so I wasn't sure if she knew how much I admired her.

So, I turn back to let her know,

"Hi there pretty lady, I've been missing you." Your smile your heart, everything that makes you, you.

She smiled back at me with such pride and said, "I knew you'd be back. I've been waiting on you."

You're my hero.

If I Don't See Tomorrow

If I don't see tomorrow,

Don't cry for me

I was blessed in this life, now I get to sit with our Father in Heaven

He's prepared a seat next to him for me

I'll get to see those that left before me

This is a journey and a destination

One day, we will all …

If I don't see tomorrow,

Please know my job was done

My physical body is at rest, look for my spiritual

I'll be in the sun

Keeping you warm

Keeping you from harm

I'm your angel now

Wings spread wide

Cousins

Love in your life is a blessing,

For your first friends are your cousins.

No matter what you call them,

Cuz, cuzin, cuzzo, or buzzin

I'm thankful for my many cousins.

We are a clan with roots that run deep

You never know where you'll bump into a cousin in the street or out the country.

Cousins, I thank you for a lifetime of love, friendship and memories.

My cousins are better than yours

Don't believe me, challenge us I bet we'll win.

Cousins

Brother

Brother, the man in your life that loves you like no other

Brother by blood

Brother by bond

Birth from the same mother

You're blessed to have a man that steps up

To hold your hand, to encourage you

That has your back

Whatever it is he'll never let you lack

A brother is a best friend, a confidant, a protector, a man that shows other men the level of love you're given so he better be able to step in

He better come correct cause a brother not playing

A brother is next in line to a father

He is taught to look out for his sister, mother, wife, and daughter, not necessarily in that order

Brothers, we thank you for all you've done and still do

From your sisters by blood or bond, we love you

The One that Got Away

So how do I take it?

I was told I was the one he let get away,

That he still loved me and thought of me everyday

I was speechless, there was nothing really, I could say.

Seems we both had different recollections of what we had

It was just sex for me, but damn it seemed he really loved me,

Should I be sad?

After thinking it over, yes, I guess, Damn my bad

He kept saying how he loved me, and he was sorry how it ended

For the life of me I couldn't remember

I knew he was my friend with benefits

To him I was the one that got away

That Snapper

Is it this snapper that caught you?

That got you tripping'?

I should have warned you about this snapper before you stuck it in

This snapper is magnificent

Comes from a line of great women, strong, smart and resilient

This snapper is a gift and curse it gives life and brings it to an end.

This snapper is sweet and succulent, has made the best men want to sin

This snapper has brought great men to their knees,

Has made men buy homes, jewels, cars and SUV's

With this snapper you walk different

It gives you an extra pep in your step, a great confidence

With this snapper he may leave, but he'll be back

That snapper has a power that they can't deny it calls them back

Come get it daddy it yours tonight.

Dedicated to Aunt Alma

Title

Title, Wife.

Title, woman he loved.

She felt like she was special because she had a title Wife

I didn't have the heart to tell her he was unhappy with her, the marriage was fake, idle and stuck. I gave him what he wanted, needed. I gave him life it was me he thought of when they fucked.

I was making him happy, giving him love, bringing him joy every day.

She had a title, Wife. I had the man, so which one of us was losing, and which one of us was winning, were my thoughts day to day.

Understand before you brag or claim that title, Wife.

That it means the same to him, and your union and your vows are intact.

You know for life, Wife.

I have a title too just not fool, I'm the woman he loves the only reason YOU still have the title that you do.

I don't want him to leave you for me unless it's done on his own. When I'm done, I send him back to you, the place you call home.

Be happy for now with your Title, Wife.

Who Taught you to be a Woman?

Who taught you what it means to be a woman? You know a lady.

Was it your mother, grandmother, aunty, or your cousin? Or did you learn in the streets, I need to know baby.

It seems there are a few lessons that you missed, a few lessons that you need.

You lack the knowledge to take care of or love yourself. You're starving yourself and that can't be.

You're drowning in a sea of self-loathing and hate.

Who taught you to be a woman? They should have told you that you're a Queen.

You're amazing you're magnificent you're great.

You're more than what's between your thighs, it's what behind your eyes that makes you a woman.

It's your beautiful mind. Who Taught you to be a Woman? It doesn't matter, never mind. Listen to me you're a gift from God, your body is a temple to only be given to someone who's deserving or not at all, celibacy is powerful.

Don't give yourself or your love away. Makem earn it!

Can a Woman raise a Man to be a Man?

Can a woman raise a man to be a man?

I tried my best to raise my son. I told him as I would do the best I can. I prayed and asked God to help me raise a good man.

I knew I would need to mold him, teach him, show him what he needed to be a man.

What I didn't know, I prayed and asked God to step in.

It has been asked many times how did you raise such a good man?

I say I don't take the credit. The man you see was raised by me with God's help.

He had his hand on him from a baby and his steps were ordered.

Greatness was his destiny.

This Society of Men

The society of men today doesn't seem like they're teaching the men coming behind them the right way

We have a generation of men not providing or protecting

Instead, they're hurt, selfish, and neglectful

So, what happens to the society or generation of men behind them?

I'm asking our fathers, brother, uncles our society of men. Stand up, step up, our new generation needs you to succeed, and they need you to win.

Girl, Can You Cook?

Girl, can you cook?

Take care of a house?

Do dishes? Laundry?

Balance a checkbook?

Or are you only worried about your looks?

It takes more than hair, nails, eyelashes, and ass to get and keep a man.

What more do you have to offer?

What's your essence of being a woman?

Girl, can you cook?

Can you take care of your family and at night, read your babies a book?

There are so many pieces to being a woman

Laying on your back is not a big deal … for a real woman

Were you taught about credit or finances?

Don't be a shame to learn sis take some classes

Girl can you cook?

Can you survive out here on your own? Or is your plan to find somebody's son to bone and take care of you while he has another woman at home.

My Hero

Grandad, you were my hero

You saved me and you didn't even know

You gave me a foundation of love and support, a great man to look up to, and making you proud was all I wanted to do

We'd sit and talk, and you'd tell me your hopes, prayers and dreams for me

I used to think wow, what a high expectation, then I'd remember the sacrifice you made for me to be me

This man with a third-grade education with more knowledge than a scholar, a hardworking man, never hustled, worked for every dollar

Granddad, you were my hero

Moon and Sun

The Moon and the sun

Do you know how significant they are?

The moon has set on a day you've made it through

The sunrise, a new day you've been blessed to see begin.

To witness two of God's most beautiful gifts, sit by the
ocean, catch the moonlight hit the water or sunset.

It's a memory you'll never forget

To witness this blessing moon up and sundown is a gift.

Between Two Hearts

What do you do when you're caught between two hearts and they're both loving you?

It was once said, "Choose the second, because if you loved the first one correct, the second one couldn't exist"

I don't feel like that's true

I know I love them both and I know they love me too

Does that make me selfish or greedy that I want them both, and I don't want to choose?

Caught between two hearts, there's a chance someone may get hurt, that we all may lose

I'm not letting go, I need them both

Fuck it, this is a bomb and I hold the detonator to ignite the fuse

KABOOM

I Can't Shield You

I can't shield you or protect you if you lie

I raised my children with these words.

To tell me the truth no matter how bad it is.

If you tell me the truth, I'll walk thru the fire for you

No matter what it is, for you I'll fight.

I'd go against a giant for you, but not if you lie.

If you lie, I can't shield you and we all lose.

I can't shield you if you lie and follow a path of bad deeds. I won't follow those steps, not in my shoes.

I can't shield you if you lie, remember not everything can be forgiven.

As much as I love you, I cant shield you if you lie, you're on your own.

Choices, Chances, Consequences

We all have the three C's

Advice from an OG

Choices, Chances, and Consequences

Was what he preached

The choices we make

By the chance we take

Equal what the consequences equate

He forgot about the three C's, he got caught up and lost site of his choices and the chances he took.

Consequence is what was left, now he is dealing with those.

Choices, Chances & Consequence

Plan, Purpose, Peace

My journey of plans that lead to my purpose that helped me find my peace

One night my pain was so great I laid crying and asked God to help me please

His reply was so clear

He said, "This is a part of your journey to your destiny, to fulfill your legacy, so stop crying and get some sleep" Rest my dear

As I slept, I dreamed I could see myself, my life

It was a light, my purpose and God's plan for me became clear

My pain and suffering were a part of a bigger picture designed by God's hand that he had painted

It was up to me to do my portion be patient and to follow God's lead

I'd fall, I'd rise I never gave up, because on that night, God showed me what was on the other side

On that night I found my peace, God had shown me what could be mine

If I followed his plan to my purpose, he'd give me my piece of peace.

Here's My Heart

Here's my heart, be careful with it

It's been broken a time or two and it took me some time to put it back together.

To heal it,

Be careful it's gently mended.

Here's my heart, I trust you with it

Your voice is calming, it soothes me it gives me comfort

A sense of security I've never known.

Here's my heart it's yours to keep safe until we grow old.

No hesitation, no reservation

Here's my heart I love you.

Peace

I've found my peace

I no longer cry, I smile

I've found my peace

It's my happy place, peace of mind

My insomnia has turned into restful sleep

I've found my Peace

When I close my eyes, I no longer see you, I see me.

The me I see is happy, living, loving, growing, healing, building.

She looks back at me, winks and said, "Sister, you are strong. We are at Peace. Shoulders back head up you'd always be with me, Peace.

The Audacity

The Audacity of me

I'm out here in these streets with someone else

Lying, creeping, and cheating

Then I break down when it's done to me, that's audacity

I raise hell and fire, demanding you be good to me, yelling all about love and loyalty

While looking you right in the face, with the scent of another man on me

I take it to the wire, Damn I'm a good liar

The Audacity of me, wanting something from you I didn't want to give

Love, loyalty, respect, happy home and kids

Shit, you had no idea you were number two on a short list

Today, I'm yours

Yesterday, I was his

The Audacity of me

One day I'll stop,

Until then, fuck it, let the mic drop

The Audacity of me

You were too good for me

You were too good for me

I never meant to hurt you

This is my sincere apology

I could never repay you for what you gave me

The love, the respect, the time, the loyalty

I wasn't in the right state to receive the blessing you were, but as the woman I am today and all I've been through, it's back in your love I prefer

A love that was patient, a love that was kind

A love that was quiet, yet simply divine

I apologize for how things ended; I want you to be happy

Last we spoke I apologized, and you seemed offended. In your cold tone you said, "I accept your apology," you were cold as ice. You said, "I took your light and altered your life."

You were too good for me

One of the few things in life I regret is hurting you, I digress.

I've prayed and I asked for your forgiveness, as you forgave me, I buried the chapter and put our past to rest

My hope for you is that you're happy, find love, have a family.

Whether you know it or not, your love made me strong.

You were too good for me

Legacy

I come from the line, the legacy of a man. A man with only a third-grade education.

A strong gentle kind man, a Witty man with a heart of gold.

Kind eyes and patience.

This man would leave behind a foundation, a legacy to stand and build on.

That I had no choice to be the woman I am today.

He had given me someone to look up to. He was my hero.

He would say baby, education is the key, and you can do anything and be anything you want to be if you work hard and believe.

I cried when he died, but I made him a promise that I'd make sure he was proud of me.

I am his Legacy.

Elbert August Murriel, My Granddaddy

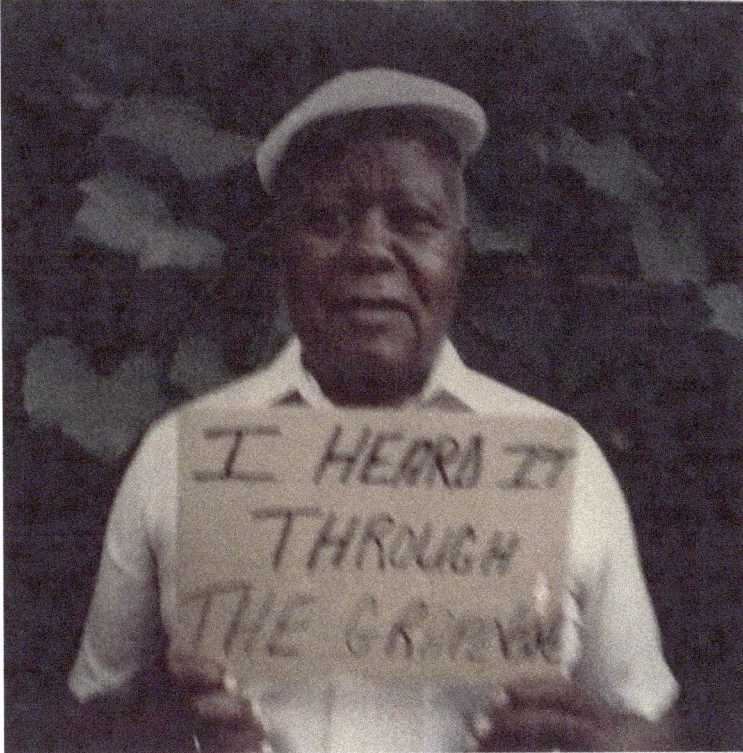

Pride, Ego, Pain, Love

Pride pride pride ego ego ego painnnnn, LOVE.

One day, listening to the rain, I started to cry.

It had suddenly hit me and from this reality I could not hide

I had a battle raging inside,

Love, ego, pain and pride.

And sadly, I just understood that these things could not exist in my heart.

Impossible to coexist, live, nor reside at the same time or I'd surely die.

Pride was a killer of my dreams

Ego is a thief of true love in my life

Pain had become a flotation device, a place to be comfortable until you die.

God touched me, opened my eyes, I grew in love

He whispered, love is the healer, the medicine, the cure that you need.

He healed my pain, took away my foolish pride

Love is stronger than any ego he taught me to lean on him & how to let go.

No more Pride Pain or Ego. Only love resides.

Soul Snatcher

"Hello, young lady, may I have a word?"

That's what I heard before I turned and there he stood,
standing there looking so fine damn I mean looking real good

As I one'd him over, naughty thoughts cross my mind,

So, I replied, "If you must," with a sly grin

He proceeded to say words, only fueled by lust

Never asked me my name or gave me his

That was red flag #1

In my mind pay attention this one here is slick boo

As I'm looking at this well-dressed, well-spoken man in his
eyes, his next words spoken were not a surprise, you see

He made me an offer of pleasure

Between the sheets, these were his words to me

He said, "Close your eyes and repeat after me,

I'm going to let you give me pleasure, in return I'm gonna let
you please me"

He proceeded with, "I'm going to suck you and kiss you from
your head to your toes, open you up, and caress your soul."

Although his words were sexy, a few issues with his offer
smelled like shit not a rose, that only a lady like the soul

snatcher could help him with she was up for the challenge little did he know

As I chuckled, he opened his eyes with a look of shock, awe and surprise

He said, "Why are you laughing? Do I make you nervous and weak?"

I said, "No way, Satan. I have the answers you seek"

I said, "Listen close, none of this you should miss

Your words came to me like a snakes' kiss nasty and vile, not soft and sweet like a lover's first kiss.

I'd like to thank you for this chance to give you some advice before we part,

My apologies for calling you Satan a short time ago.

Although the title seemed fitting, since you're out here snatching souls.

Although your offer was cute, I must gracefully decline

My soul is taken as well as my body and mind.

I keep thinking to myself, how could you be A soul snatcher?

If you're out here snatching souls, why don't you have your own woman to please?"

He stood there, mesmerized, breathing slowly, his sly grin had faded

He was calm but look deflated

I was elated.

I am a woman of substance

Not easily impressed by your seductive words and nice style of dress.

My soul is not for the taking, not by you

It requires a higher level of stimulation.

On that note I'll say my goodbyes

So, the next time you run that line, think first and remember today, the day you got your soul snatched with words by a beautiful woman with a beautiful mind.

Dereliction of Duty

There should never be a dereliction of duty when you love someone, and they need you.

Either you stand like a man, handle the duties at hand or you fold like a fan and tuck your tail between your legs and run.

There should never be a dereliction of your duty when you're the head of the family and they need you to live, to survive & to eat

There should never be a dereliction of duty when you say you love someone, and you know they need you.

You have defaulted on the promise to lead love and protect

You have only yourself to blame for the outcome of your life today

And the absence of love in your life due to your own neglect

Look at that man in the mirror ask him, "how can I lead my family again?"

Scream Dereliction of duty is my sin in your own mind you're a legend.

The Family Among Us

Be thankful for the family among us, no two souls are the same. Be thankful for the family among us, for tomorrow is not promised so love on them today. Yesterday is gone and we may never cross paths again.

Be thankful for the family among us, our elders and their wisdom has given us knowledge and strong foundation from their sacrifice and pain.

The history of love and guidance to break a generation of curses, to give us the fortitude to see our families prosper, and our histories never to be repeated.

Be thankful for the family among us, that our lives will get better with every passing day, we create better days for our future generations, before we pass away.

Be thankful for the family among us, lets create traditions and build a heathy strong family grounded in love that will span many, many, many lifetimes.

I am thankful for the family among us.

You Dare Dream?

Do you dare dream?

Do you dare dream of the possibilities of what could be?

All the goals you could accomplish, the heights and pinnacles you could reach. Glass ceilings breaking, the force of nature that you are the heat under your feet.

If only you would dare to dream and believe you could succeed.

Don't overthink just move one foot in front of the other, breath, blink, then leap.

Dig deep, now close your eyes and imagine what could be, if you follow your dreams.

Yourself belief with faith, vigor and zeal if you dare to dream and work hard

It's there over the horizon on the other side of the hill.

Do you dare to dream?

Her Love made me believe I could do anything

Thank you to all who have supported me throughout this journey. I am humbled and so appreciative of your love and words of encouragement. I was able to make this, and my other books come to fruition because you all believed in me. To my family, especially my children, my friends, my Love and my mentor JB.

I am because you all are...

Love you all to infinity

Thank you,

Felicia Nicole